Poetry Nook

Popular Contest Winners

Plum White Press

Published by Plum White Press LLC

For information concerning reprints, email: admin@poetrynook.com

ISBN-13:	978-1939832139
ISBN-10:	1939832136
LOC PCN:	2016949209
BISAC:	Poetry / Anthologies

Cover design copyright © 2016 by Plum White Press LLC

Cover image from "Le Concert champêtre" by Jean-Baptiste-Camille Corot, 1857, via Wikimedia Commons. Public domain.

Published in the United States of America

Table of Contents

Poetry Nook

Popular Contest Winners

Hands and Feet

Rod E. Kok

Put your hand in mine
I whispered to
my newborn son
I'll try to keep you
safe and warm

Put your hand in mine,
together we will fight.

Let me carry you, my boy
for your feet are weary,
even though they have never
carried a load.

Lend me your hand,
dear Michael,
for once you are gone,
I will see your prints
on my heart.

Walk with me
in memory,
dear child.
For someday,
we will walk
together.

Put your hand in mine,
and bid us farewell.

Lay quiet, my baby boy
Jesus will take you
home.

Beyond Skirts and Dapper Things

Johann F. Potgieter

Consider: lovers sitting in the stairwell.
He calls her by her name, Dolores;
she has her fingers coiled within his curls -
blithe for the fruit she bears,
that, in bearing, will cause the bough to snap!

Before all this he dreamt of fame,
and now wonders (as her eyes are counting rain):
"you think too soon we spoiled your pearls?"
And they wonder if she cares...
Blithe - for there is little else that they can do.

And all along, there, Time had toiled,
as they slept, folded, into morrow;
carving into granite, dust and bone-meal falling,
HERE LIES THE MAKINGS OF A GILDED SORROW -
FALLEN FRUIT FEEDS NOT THE STREET

Blithe... For such is Time's most ancient calling.

Book of life

vandecaf

The sharp pages
Of her presence
Cut his fingers
With each turn

That blood
Is the ink
In which their
Future is learned

Previously published on Twitter (@van_decaf)

Urania (Italian)

Εὐρυδάμας

I

Era chiamata
"Urania"
dagli dei!

E io ...

... io ero
La sua Luna!

Lei era me—
ed io ...
ero lei,

... in un'altra
vita,

in un'altra era.

II

Alla sua nascita
Cantarono
inni sacri

Lodi!

riecheggiarono
In quel giorno

Nei cuori
Di tutti
i saggi—

Dolcemente
sussurravano

"Urania!"

III

La sua
bellezza:
suprema—

Raggiante!

Tuttavia le Parche
Gelose

Cloto
Lachesi
Atropo

Tagliarono
Il filo d'oro

Della mia Urania!

IV

Lei morì
In gioventù
Pallida, bella

Urania!

Me la
rubarono

la posero a
riposare alle
Porte Di Ishtar

E l'oscurità
Cadde sopra

La Terra.

Ourania (English Translation)

Εὐρυδάμας

I

She was called
"Ourania"
by the Gods!

and I...

...I was
Her Moon!

still she was
me and I
her,

...in another
Lifetime,

Ages hence...

II

At her birth
They sang hymns
of praise!

Anthems

that echo
to this very day

On the hearts
of all the
Wise—

Softly
whispering...

"Ourania!"

III

Her beauty
was beyond
measure—

Radiant!

Yet the fates
grew jealous;

Clotho
Lachesis
Atropos

cutting short
the golden cord

of my Ourania

IV

She died
fair of face;
in youth

Ourania!

they stole
Her away—

laying her
to rest at the
Gates of Ishtar

and darkness
fell upon

the land

Eve (and us three)

Johann F. Potgieter

even in its light the night's dark shades
still painted swaths along our sea –
our conversation ebbed carelessly and tired,
creeping up along the beach,
each of us settled on this bench named Eve.

some lamp above our minds flickered undecided
in the wake of our impatience for morning.
some ellipse of geese gave the dawn its perforations
as the curious air beckoned our relations.

distinct was the absence of vacant reassurances;
in grunts and nods our speech and understanding.
quite readily we'd speak of sex,
guessing where the sun would rise.

I had run my fingers along our bodies -
still and quietly arranged in perfect geometry
on your bed.
but this was long ago.

for now the ocean pulled its tides back home,
and with it the residue of a yesterday that died.
for the lady of our discontent had peaked beyond the curl,
and the riptides reminisced the boy they drowned just hours ago.
right then we did not know... he was our age.

gentle patience

Rick Stassi

Guardian eye, strict ray of light,
Protecting vessels adrift at night.
Whilst commanding swells pound the shore,
Offering featherlight droplets upon the moor.
I am one who spies things pass
From warmly within forgiving glass.
Wondering always, my thoughts abound,
As the laden sea air, my tears find the ground.
Sky obscured by phantom mist
Am I a vessel poised to list?
Askew I seem as waves overwhelm,
Begging sweet guardianship at the helm.
Lighthouse, now, radiant toward me
The paradise drama unfolds to see.
And I, this vessel, drift not as before,
God's gentle patience surrounds me once more.

Eros

Johann F. Potgieter

today casts the hue of happiness
into the ocean, into the waves;
into the languid motion of leaves
of grass and palm trees waving.
diviners of clouds would look
pointedly at the piano-like stillness
of the cumulus harbingers of joy.
serenity would birth itself in sunlight.

and I'll be Psyche -
slumbering in the shade.

Handbag

Suzanne Kosmerl

A rock
a car
Darth Vader
chocolate chip granola bars
a rubber band ball
half-empty wipes
a few stray raisins
chewed gum
and a broken stick.
Once,
my handbag held
a book
a compact
ticket stubs
thick black eyeliner
a bright red lipstick
clean tissues
a full address book
fresh gum
and a little perfume.

Counterclockwise

Raunthu

I dream counterclockwise sometimes
Cherry blossom petals lifting from the desert soil
Like gentle snowflakes
An island, a church, a trees lane, a vast field in America
No distance

We're both getting flowered on
As you're picking petals and sprinkling them on my hair

You've always been there in those dreams
Since tomorrow, when I will be born

I open my eyes
Find a cherry scented petal in my hair

And remember there is no pause
This dream is.

- True
Since eternity.

enjoying moments

Rick Stassi

pre-dawn melody
from atop a tree - announcing
new things arriving
that soon I shall see.

the sun grabs the horizon
with his hands an arising pull
up to peek upon new lands
and break a sleepy lull.

the flow of a song intertwined
with the stroke of a brush
a new melodic picture
to linger in - mind not to rush.

Labour Club

Paul Cotterill

Beaming faces, floral dresses
Sunday suits, with rakish hats on young 'uns
Posing for the picture
Before the charabanc

To Blackpool
Rock and solidarity
A stroll along the prom

A pint, or two
Bitter, brown
Workers, comrades, friends

Evening time, the sun glows red and shoulders pink
The bus rumbles through the unlit roads
Sing songs become snores

Remembered
From grainy prints
Stacked to go
White van will come tomorrow

The Labour club
Bare patches on the wall from hanging years

The Labour club
Liquid dreams of comrades gone

The Labour club
One nation
Liquidation

Note: Non-UK readers may wish to know that Blackpool is a seaside town in North West England, now fallen on harder times since the growth of budget arilines to mainland Europe, but once a popular holiday and day trip destination for people from the industrial towns across the North.

Oh, and a white van in the UK is associated with cheap clearances and removals.

L.U.S.T.

Lexi Davis

Boy, lust me so good.
I could convince myself it's love,
I know better, but it's so good
When you lust me so hard.
Find myself dazed off without warning,
Remembering every touch and expression.
Biting my lip as if you're in front of me,
Taking my body into yours and lusting
What we are could be sin
When the night of last was better
Than your last, all you can do is hope,
Hope the high lasts.
Want you watch, watch as I gas myself up with my own lust?
I know you like a show.
I just want you to lust me,
Forget love its side effects.
Be my drug.
My high.
My downfall.
Damage me.
Turn me into a monster.
Tear my apart with this sin.
Lust me like you want, do what you want.
My body, your hostage.
Your passion, the weapon.
Take it all into your being, die for it.
Come back and seek revenge.
Murderous and treacherous being who you are.
Lust me. Forget love. I want your lust,
More than anything.

VICTORIA

Bob Rodriguez

The past, without which there would be no now.

Brings forth a soul to ease those ill with strife.

Gives of herself as much as hearts allow.

And meets the man who she shall join as wife.

The two embark on that journey so dear.

At first, they two alone to climb the hill.

And then two pilose friends so loved appear.

'T'would seem the tale complete, word not, for quill.

Then, lo, the visit of one Gabriel.

Almost on the very same day of name.

From the heavens the prime to cry, now fell.

And word of the arrival did proclaim.

There is but one that shall be called the first.

None else shall ever be so likewise nursed.

Reciprocation

Ebonee Eleby

her hands too full of the giving to receive, he became accustomed to the
taking. the forever full well of all she worked to become. never could
imagine it was fault of him. her shrinking. his growing. felt she wasn't
made for his stature, too small of a woman for a man like him. convinced
himself she was too frail to handle the weight. feet steady she stood. open
palmed, closed mouthed. taught to be all her man needs, regardless of
the emptying. "that's role you were born to play." mama said, "men will
be men & women will be all else. expect nothing from a man that has
shown you all of him." first time soon she'll hear her voice again, feel the
hunger again. pains be catalyst, be the thunder that shakes loose lazy love.
blessed be the rain for the coating. the silk that settles on skin, these days
she be her own well wishes.

firefly

Rick Stassi

dark and frail,
gray hanging on to
a bit of white
lest a black demise.
overcast skies absorbing
what sunlight it can
waiting for night
and equanimity of hue.
pinpoint light hidden
well within my soul
shrouded in clouds
screaming to be heard
playing with the thought
that even a firefly
can be a lantern
in his small domain...
can I?

Bhavacakra

Johann F. Potgieter

he hung his hands through window bars
and cursed the street so that it knew
she sung her tune with cracked up lips
and cursed them all and pursed her lips
to whistle down the street she went
those sordid tunes her mind had lent

first the school bell
then the steeple's
then the woman selling wires
and the flyers in the gutters
as if the gutters would know best

he flung his hands upon the sky
and wrung it as to wring it dry
he wore their curses on his feet
and knew that one day they would meet
as fathers, mothers, sisters, brothers
or stars and leaves and quiet things

and in the street
two tourists standing
unaware that they are lost
then the gunshot, the silence
and a whistling woman's tune

Where Sweetness Lies

B. Flynn

Perhaps it is a fool who dreams
Of ripened fruit before
The seed inspires

But it is wrong to quiet the heart
When it has seen
Where sweetness lies

Then soften its voice to whisper
No more than laughter
As but a smile

Said of wonder and endless time
Past and future oft
At Janus' door

So as to question of our claim
This field would bare
A fruitless fall

Leave me then, as I lay here
With care and grace begot
By blissful stare

Nimisha

FABIYAS M V

In her layette, she looked fair.
'Nimisha', the parents called her.
When aged five, the polio plucked
the strings that her legs moved.
As a stringless violin, her legs rest.
In the wheelchair, she grows up
along with her mother's tension
and the father's anxieties.

The rustic children wish her,
but nobody takes her
to the festival
in a shrine rural.
She wears new dress
but as the butterflies in her frock,
she also cannot flit
to the shrine yard.

Cough waves, today also,
shake her lungs so.
The distant drumbeats and the holy music
move her fingers in the wind rhythmic.
The clarion does resonate and ripple
the divine thoughts in her ears.
She never knew
pneumonia packing her soul.

Serenity of the twilight collapses,
as, again, the drum storm develops.
Few knew Nimisha swooned.
Later, the people intoned,
'Being holy,
an apt day it is.'
In emptiness infinite,
her parents knew her truly.

Poem #463

Julia Katherine Carrigan

Just a poem
Just one in four hundred sixty three
What is one in four hundred sixty three?
What significance is one?
Not just a poem, Anything, Everything
Just one more
Just another grain of sand on the beach
To be taken away by the wind soon
To be forgotten
To be discarded
To be looked at years later with a laugh
One more poem in a collection of hundreds
What makes it stand out?
Only characteristics all the others can match
What is the meaning of its existence?
It's not important
It won't be remembered
Why not just take one out
One grain taken from the beach does not matter at all
But without it 462
If you were to erase one, Why not them all?
Because, without the sand there is no beach
462 is not a number really
It's just 462 separate 1s
A beach is not a beach just lots of sand
One in four hundred sixty three, is how it has to start
You may be one in millions but, you are one and that's all a million is

season of darkness

Rick Stassi

I dreamed about a December morn
When life was drawn and cold forlorn
Doubting pleasure's full embrace
In somber slumber's selfish pace.
Ice and frost did slow my gait
Longer evenings embodied fate
The sun slipped so fast away
Over horizon for another's day.
The sorrow watching measured moments
I totter now upon deciding fence.
In whose world shall I fall?
Not haunting emptiness, the worst of all...
But the sun ascends in veiled rise
Shattering darkness warming eyes
I fear the light its revealing ways
Vulnerable heart feels warm rays.
This is my time out of stillness reborn
Trapped by years of masked forlorn
Upon the face of God I now look upon
December morn soon is gone.

43

BryceH

Pin up my love with clothes pins. Display me
on billboards on the side the road. I'm the old
supermarket, the abandoned furniture store
that we smoke in front of. I have a dream
of the following statements:

All people will have a name of their choosing.
All people will drive cars to imagination.
Ask if this is a headache or a possession
before taking medicine.
Ignominious replacements for alternatives.
Sky and starstruck, the replacements for parks
and compartments.
My love in the glovebox.
Rubber bands around my feelings.

Pine my love. Display me on you.
Smoking into the darkness, the angels
in the streetlights keening. Strumming on
the strings of our love. Spinning in the night.
Wheels turning in darkness.

I have found the stars in your eyes.

The Road

B. Flynn

Come in, she whispered,
  and called me her dear.

It's by no strange chance
  that you are now here.

Take off your boots,
  dry your feet by the fire,

Where I will cook for you
  should it be your desire.

Let my hands work first
  over those frozen bones

And comfort the soul
  that has been out alone.

Your strength will return
  not long after you've ate,

But the sun is low now
  and the road can wait.

Feeling truly safe there
  I stepped into her door.

At once I was certain
  that I had stood there before.

All things were familiar
  in the ways that she moved;

A truth in her kindness
  which need not be proved.

Now wrapped in the warmth
  that she gave of herself,

Reminded a lost heart
  of how good it once felt.

She drew a bit closer
  then my spirit was moved.

My face had been warmed
  while my fingers were soothed.

I looked into her eyes
  that were deep and serene,

They shone with a brightness
  only once I had seen.

Men have oft been inspired
  by eyes such as hers.

I too, was so captured
  for as long as it were.

A long journey remained
  but the hour was late;

My eyes had grown heavy
  So the road would wait.

Qaphela (Afrikaans and isiZulu)

Johann F. Potgieter

qaphela – there is fire here
in my indlovukazi's eyes
she burns with her umbuso
plakkerskamp op mitchelsplein
qaphela – there is a fire in the cape
and there's an ember in her heart
that died

hier vertoef 'n vlammeman
in my keel – op my tong
op die berg en in die see
thetis, are you not mamlambo
you serpent in the rivers
did you know that there is fire
here

oh indlovukazi of old
her braids adorned
with shells
and beads
on a poster that reads:
"guided township tours"

Qaphela (English Translation)

Johann F. Potgieter

beware – there is fire here
in my high queen's eyes
she burns with her kingdom
the shanty town on mithcelsplein
caution – there is a fire in the cape
and there's an ember in her heart
that died

sojourning here, a thing of flames
within my throat
upon my tongue
on the mount and in the sea
thetis, are you not mamlambo
you serpent in the rivers
did you know that there is fire
here

oh royalty of old
her braids adorned
with shells
and beads
on a poster that reads:
"guided township tours"

Found

Steve Shultz

I found myself in a slumber
wiping wonder from my tired eyes
bear-hugging blackness
arm wrestling badgers
playing tag with the monster
underneath the stairs;
I found myself tongue kissing rolling thunderheads
climbing trees, stretching fingers
to catch bolts of lightning
soothed by sirens, not seeking shelter
looking up in hailstorms, mouth agape
swallowing the largest stone;
I found myself glaring at the sun
eating handfuls of dirt
mowing lawns barefoot
savoring each burr & goathead
pierce my heel, between my toes;
I found myself freeing butterflies
giving away miscellanea
seeking out crowds
shaking unwashed hands
opening my house to strangers;
I found myself on a zipline
high above the tree line
raising my voice, arguing a point;
In throes of passion
I found myself cage fighting death herself
adding her own head
to the string around her neck

The Love Tree

Kalyana Hapsari

Shall I scratch out your name on our love tree?
The tree is sick, our love has turned into a sad plight.
Shall I cut the tree down at once and burn the root?
The blossoms reek wounds, infested with gloom.

Don't wait for winters, it hardly survives the spring,
where the sun nurtures, the wind is light and caring.
Too many fruits are never a burden for a tree,
but too much love is often too much to bear.

Some clouds that are heavy with rain
shall immediately pour out their pain.
Some eyes that can no longer hold tears
must make the cheek a path for those rolling shears.

The quiet breeze shall now be a broken love's spell.
The bleak looking moon is where our lost hopes dwell.
I beg the Grim not to take our love's life,
but he warns me not to challenge his might.

Now, I need not scratch out your name.
The tree itself is vanishing.

Cataclysmia

BruiseViolet

Tidal waves are coming, spread wide across the ocean,
& there's smoke in the distance from forest fires burning

But that water, it can't reach them. It is of no assistance
& all will turn to ash, it'll only take an instance.

Swallow up the coast, carry the ashes far away;
Bodies of the dead, love letters, tears & decay.

Float back to the sea, mix with oil spills & carnage.
Deselecting nature, poisoned lakes choked with garbage.

Black holes are being torn in the universe,
Tornadoes, hurricanes... it only gets worse.

The ice shelves are melting, drown the wonders of the land.
Great floods in the deserts, no more castles in the sand.

Earthquake tremors raging, split open the crust,
Walls are collapsing, degrade our bodies to dust.

Some say global warming, it's a "natural" disaster,
But Hell knows when it ends, because it does not matter.

Praying to the Heavens, looking up to the sky
But acid rain's falling, UV radiation, burn your eyes.

& meteors are coming, hurdling at cataclysmic rates,
Leaving fear 'n destruction in their great cosmic wakes.

Disintegrating structures, rusting shells of burnt out cars.
Nuclear implosions, supernovas, fallen stars.

Volcanoes spewing lava, infernos burning bright.
Now how long will that money keep you warm at night?

We're killing one another with war & acts of violence,
While our children are left starving, suffering in silence.

Diseases running rampant, viral plagues, drug resistance,
With species decimation- erasing our existence.

Lady Liberty chastised by divine light.
Crucified lovers lusting in the night.

Lightning storms are brewing, speed forward hands of time.
Armageddon's coming to end this circus ride.

& Earth, she'll solve this mathematical imbalance
Back to equilibrium with her natural talents.

Because life, (when we're gone) will flourish once again,
Rectify injustice, & forgive us for the pain.

Holidaying in Chimney Woods

FABIYAS M V

Holidaying in Chimney Woods
These woods are like a mother
                     putting all embers out.
Sweet wind winnows me out of
                       all secret worries.
As I dip myself into the woody stream,
                  tension termites disappear.
Throats of birds broadcast unceasing songs
                    like our FM station.
When a tribesman squeezes a honey-comb, I
               ride my tongue up the palm.
My mind convalesces slowly here
                   under the foliage.
Fireflies fly out through the windows
                     of my skull.
Fresh thoughts are cooked in the seclusion
                 of the woods.
Shoots of dreams reappear, breaking the dried
               pods of my memory.
I see the fossils of a paradise, which we had lost
               under the past.

The Time Apart

B. Flynn

Heavy on me now she pulls
As distance starts to grow
Yet quickly in my mind I see
Her lines I've come to know

I let her go amidst belief
At our centers we are bound
All orbits have their farthest reach
Then come faster back around

One last kiss is ours to hold
Until it blooms anew
The time apart is useful then
To look at what we grew

Would I for her my secrets bare
My soul into the light
And still her fondness unto me
Keep by in her sight

A fire needs its space to burn
To hold its scarlet heat
The time apart is good for flame
And hearts that singly beat

Cherishing the words she speaks
Numbered in my mind
Happiness around them kept
With smile I will find

The time apart is like the wind
It ushers us to move
Gently but in sudden squall
And to a place that's true

To whom shall thanks be given for
A gift that has a name
A name I whisper silently
'Ere the time apart is came

Gogyoshi Prelude

Johann F. Potgieter

beyond the
intimacy
of the floor
my sentiments
are revolving

Vignette

Lexi Davis

Skies so blue, I mean black; ominous
Yet, I smile at the sight of you
Though you're nowhere close
Only your essence lingers.
How do you miss a soulless soul?
Holding on to what was promised,
Guaranteed. Written. Printed.
Opposite results.
Up all night, sleep all day.
Insomniac. Low energy. Hyped. High.
My mind running faster than your lies.
Guess this is what they would call Vignette.

Hello World

Julia Katherine Carrigan

Hello World

Nice to see you today!
Hope everything is going well
Hope it's going your way
Hope the sun is feeling bright
The sky still looks blue
I feel ready for today
How about you?

Hello World
It's already almost noon
I'm hungry for lunch
It should be ready soon
The birds are sounding cheerful
I see a smile on your face
So far all is swimmingly
You do your job with such grace

Hello World
The night has come once again
I will soon rest head and leave the washing to the rain
In the land of dreams where I take flight and fly
I see to many reasons to live for and so little for to die
Soaring so high as I look down at life
There is so much love there and yet so much strife
As I drift off to sleep I whisper a few words
See you tomorrow
Goodnight World

Horizon

Rick Stassi

a breeze and a sigh now
each grasping at your
inquisitive uncertain being
within your shadows
your sighs expel things
enamored yesterday
but cast out today
under a new light
the breeze beckons
and pushes you to places
unseen but trusted
in tomorrow's eyes
your spirit sways
gently about in waves
of hope and forgiveness
-breezes and sighs
and you see azure
skies kissed by
viridian seas at the
point of forever

The Long Coming Back (part 3)

B. Flynn

I hope
you will remember
all the Good
that we have shared
Good
that might not have happened
if
none of us
had dared
It might be painful
for a time now
but I know that you will heal
and as this old ship
is sinking
low
hold tight against the keel
I hope
that you can
see the light you gave me
Still shining
against the black
that is all
that is left of me now
there is no
coming back

Legacy

FABIYAS M V

It's the sole legacy from his dad.

A cup of ice cream tempts him
more than the alluring face of
a fair lady. Eating is his ecstasy
forgetting the existence.

It blooms in orange or red hue
in a test tube in the summer
of tension.

Urinary impulse usually slices
his sleep into three at night.

Nameless anxieties burn in his
mind. Fatigue remains in the ash.

Sugar syrup flows through his veins
and rusts his internal engines.

His doctor's stethoscope listens
money-beats. Pharmacy sells him
new complications. Insulin leads
him to the blind alley.

He sloshes in the sludge of life,
reaching nowhere.

Sanoj's a writer - his rating is high
in a glucose meter. Sooner or later
he will be awarded with
the silence of a coma.

Photos

Julia Katherine Carrigan

Photos are peculiar things
Memories on strange paper
Patterns of ink to remember one day
One day out of a million
People take pictures of everything
Extraordinary and normal
Faces of people we see every day
Faces we've never seen before
Nature and Cities
Nature in Cities
Photos of Photos
And photos of those
Photos in black and white and grey and whites and a copperish tone
Photos in color but black as the dark
You can look at photos and transport to different times and places
One day we will transport to this moment
So say Cheese

Mangoes in Early Fall

Shauna Osborn

There's no civilized way to eat some fruits--
just savage sucking & ripping of flesh,
the large white seed in the center
waiting to be exposed. Bite into it
like an apple or a peach--such sweetness
drips down the throat, blonde fibers
much like corn silk & just as uneatable.
This exotic tropical fruit--only seen in
romantic comedies located in some
exotic place--never grown amongst
the pear trees & grape vines. & when
the large white seed with remaining amber
mohair is put on the plate with the
toughened shaved skin (read rind)
that couldn't be chewed, the poem is done
gone, left in the space of time that can only
be broken with teeth marks through inviting
red/green flesh

first published in *Cultural Weekly*

Cold Blooded

Lexi Davis

Rapid breathing matching my heart rate.
Rubbing my eyes, over and over again,
Nothing in my view changes.
Everything is slowed as if in the freezing process.
I search around for some sort of clue of a dream.
Pixelation, a focus point of an escape route, anything.

Nothing.

Despite the deceleration of my surroundings,
The world spins faster as time soars.
The things I once loved, ceased to exist.
It was stopped and dropped.
Forgotten about just like that.
I lose it.

I've lost it all.

The sun turned into the moon in more than one way.
The warmth was replaced by a cold hand.
Shivering to understand whilst questioning, yet,
No answer. No solution nor probable cause.
Hunger within had to react and hunt.
Vampire it was, it smelled blood.

Teeth stained with the crimson sin.

The sound had deafen my inner thoughts
But heighten my outer relative fear.
I could no longer live a fantasy or lie.
Lie for a greater good about a heart that stopped beating,
A long time ago.
My only option to regain partial fantasy
Was the very thing that ended it.

No weapon formed against me shall...

Prosper?
What if it wasn't I it was formed against?
Now I'm standing in the middle of what was my life.
My life inside of another life.

As the loved I needed creates rivers beneath me.
Unlike my Creator, I sunk below, drowning in despair.

Give me the ability to accept change.

That appears to be out of my hands entirely.

That meant I'd have to live with memories and not touches.

Give me the ability to live. As my life source has returned home.

Robins

Arabella Wraye

Sharp, swift flight
aching, breathtaking,
against slate sky
ebb and flow to the feast
faux cedar, living bird feeder
Below the cacaphony and fanfare,
my ying-yang cat sits and stares,
moodily,
into the distance.....
as if such avian antics are below
and not above
her, and
so far out of reach.
But, deep in her little kit kat heart,
where kittenish ways still paw,
starfish, biscuit,
the place where purrs come from
(and what are purrs, after all?
but the resonance of remembrances
rubbing together as the rise.)
Hidden here, with purrs paused,
the secret wish rises,
that she,
too,
had wings.

guess how well I slept

John Reinhart

camping
with my two sons
ages 3 and 4 1/2
in our yard
as our fire expired
we were treated
to what felt like
a personal fireworks show
then, snuggled together,
we pondered owls and bats,
drifting into belated restlessness
called sleep
by ten Mattheus slept peaceably
while Lucien tossed, turned, snored,
and woke, until 6:30: "Papa, can we
sleep in the tent again tonight?"

A Crab Scuttles Across The Velvety Mustard Sand, And Disappears Into The Sea Foam

skylarlynch

Upon the golden eve at morn
A sailor floats upon the shore
And eagle's beak do burn the sun
Where phoenix feathers sprout
And wave upon a frothy wave
Do scuttle to and fro
And midnight rock do hold acrock
Where cocker shells may grow

Brighid

Mary Soon Lee

Six years old,
youngest of the demon's servants,
didn't cry when the king
roused her after the demon's death;
nor when, an hour later, she remembered
the cut-off scorched scream
her dad gave, aflame;
nor when, towards evening,
a fishmonger recognized her
and offered to see her back to her aunt;
nor when, weeks later, the fishmonger
delivered her to her aunt, who hugged her --
and hugged the fishmonger --
and wept.

That night the farm tomcat,
a gray and surly mouser
not inclined to affection,
lay down on Brighid's blanket
and matter-of-factly licked her arm,
her bare shoulder, her face,
his rough tongue rasping her skin,
and she cried,
thinking not of her dad,
or their burnt home, their burnt town,
but of her mother's voice,
a voice she'd forgotten
until the demon borrowed it,
that she'd known to be a lie
but followed anyhow.

First published in Apex Magazine.

Leonardo's Cat

Susan427

In a sunlit place
she lounged in style,
Desdemona the Siamese.

So in a rush
he took his brush,
as she took her ease

and painted her smile
on a human face.

The Works

John Reinhart

Last night I wrote a symphony –
"Corrugated Recycles" I call it –
on the back of a pizza box.

It starts with strings playing pizzicato,
lumbers deep into horns covered in grease,
then cymbals, like giant pepperoni, crash.

The second movement creeps up the side
onto the top: "Cosmic Pizza" is all percussion,
rise and expansion, sustain, rest.

Movement three goes inward,
the most obscure and difficult part,
cluttered with crust and crumbs, real cheese,

stains too dark, too somber for any but celli,
summoning aged wood
like twelve year barreled bourbon.

Finally, up the inside lid, closure,
a simple melody to light the tunnel –
done in thirty minutes or it's free.

(first published in 94 Creations Journal #6)

Cyberstalking

Rie Sheridan Rose

In cyberspace no one can hear
you scream...
as you show your plastic
mask to the online world.
"SlicOperatur" your moniker,
cruising for a rush.
Razor wit slicing nubile mindsets
on middle-aged thrill seekers.
It's all mind games...
all good fun till someone
puts an email out.
You congregate in chat rooms
afraid to face real bodies
when there are avatars
to be manipulated.
Stalking less personal
but packing no less punch.
Poison pens translated
to pecked out pixels,
but biting as hard.
Striking in the heart of
the internet...
big game hunters separating
mice and men.

(Previously published in the chapbook *By Candlelight*.)

Some Notes of a Religious Nature

Bill Cushing

Jesus was sent
to die for our sins
just like some package
from UPS.

He delivered the goods
to humanity,
and we delivered Him
back to Heaven

battered, beaten,
mutilated.
Some creation
we turned out to be.

The Dao of Scrabble™

Terrie Leigh Relf

bag filled with smooth squares
letters and numbers
all lead either somewhere
or nowhere--both somewhere and nowhere

there are no absolutes
dissolve the antidote
with the poison
the poison with the antidote
they are the same and yet not the same

a vowel is not a consonant
but without it
the consonant may have no meaning
this is the way of scrabble
the way of meaning-making

the way of long into the night
when the moon hangs just so in the night sky
where crickets scrape out their song
the clickclickclick of word formation
the glideclickclick of† meaning making
the clatterclatterclink of tiles in a bag

as they walk labyrinths of meaning
the 10,000 blessings are these words
these words remind us to breathe through the night
these words that breathe us so that we may breathe

clickclickclickclick
clickclickclickclick

wild parrots screeching
on the electric wire at dawn
and what to do with three Ls and a Z

END

Previously published in *Origami Condom*, 3 Nov 08

a sketch in autism: morning ritual disrupted

Lynn Tait

hot circle bursts open throws brightness through clear square in sleeping place walls throb color the me of me sways in and out waves of hurt snake around my paper coat the mother has touched the mother voice echoes sound upon sound scratching the hard insides that keep me from melting led to place where smell become shapes in mouth see round cup white water rains on brown specks noisy in mouth like smashing rocks SHINY SHOVEL IS WRONG bells ring THUD slam into hardness round top of me where eyes are not where soft strings are i pull with stars living on the sticks i do not walk on THUD THUD almost there place where bright turns dull sound turns off seeing turns soft voice moves like green on wood shovel now has face on end the mouse that lives in the talking box all things rest neatly now like bent cloth the mother forms sounds that mean – fill me up face splits open mickey zooms up close with eyes that tell me everything.

Ascent Aspirations; Disorders Anthology (2012)

Abominable Punctuation

John Reinhart

craters
mark the sentence left to mystery –
black eyes staring from the snowstorm
twinkling empty promises to all
but the intrepid believers
pursuing their beastly author
if only to prove his existence
as civilization brought Grendel
to his knees and raised the digital
totem to ward off the legends
of footprints in the snow…

(originally published in *Star*Line* http://sfpoetry.com/starline.html)

Oh, Wind...

Rie Sheridan Rose

I cannot follow you today...
Though you caress my cheek
And whisper promises.

Your touch a welcome thing
As the jealous sun beats down
From his high seat.

I cannot follow you today...
My heart downcast by care and worry,
Though you tease my hair and beckon.

I imagine the delights we'd share
As you led me forward to adventure.
But duty bids me stay confined.

Watching through glass
As you gambol through the trees.
Oh, Wind...I cannot follow you today.

A Girl Who Sells Peanuts

FABIYAS M V

She floats on the saffron shore
holding a bamboo basket.
Her heart beats
within the shelter
of peanut shells.

Toys and text books,
picnics and pamperings;
all collided on a wall,
but death dropped her
to be tossed.

The girl in a dirty frock –
she sells parched peanuts
for coins and eye-pricks.
'Peanuts', 'Peanuts' –
her withered call haunts
her parents in the grave.
Her pale figure walks away
with Time Teacher.

My Neighbor's Cthulhu

Josh Brown

My neighbor's Cthulhu pooped on my lawn again. He denied it; said it was the pomeranian from across the street. But do pomeranians crap green toxic sludge that kills the grass and burns a fucking hole in the ground? I think not. Keep your damn Cthulhu on a leash. My neighbor's wood fence is scorched and smashed to pieces. I don't think it is doing much good keeping his Cthulhu in. I couldn't sleep last night; I was up late listening to the screams, howls, and blood-curdling shrieks of my neighbor's Cthulhu. I was late for work the next morning because I came outside to my driveway and discovered I had a flat tire. I just know that damn Cthulhu was humping my truck again. My neighbor of course denied that, too. Every time I turn around, there it is, that damn Cthulhu. I'm consumed by grim visions; the voices inside my head are like a drumbeat, terrifying tentacles trying to punch their way out. My eyes are crying blood. All because of my neighbor's damn Cthulhu.

Daddy's Girl

Jamey Bibbee

If I could see you again ...
Could I walk in and kiss you with no words
No questions asked - no lies told
Could we just love each other ...
In my arms - could it be you that I hold
I love you after all the tears and the pain
True love never dies - Forever it will remain

Do you ache for me the way I do for you
This happened for a reason - I know that much is true
But why did it have to separate me - from you

I'll never understand why all the hurt came that year
I'll be missing someone forever that much seems clear
First I was without him and now I am without you
I love you both - Couldn't you love him too

I always enjoyed being your little girl
Will I ever see you again in this world

You had a birthday this last month. I hope you are doing well
We are all doing fine - except for what happened - that's hell
I guess I'd just like my cake and eat it too
That is to be with him but also to be with you

It's been 3 years this month since I saw you last
Will it be forever - with you do I only have the past

I pray that you will accept and serve the Lord Jesus Christ
For all our sins and hurts He has already paid the price
I pray too that I receive His healing from this awful grief
He took that to the cross as well - just for me to have relief

I'm happy most days - God is really good
Today though I miss you -
Just the way "Daddy's Girl" would

Out of Orbit

John Reinhart

with sullen glances
they tolerate
our indiscretions,
the flitting trees
and fickle wind,
sitting silently
in communion
with comets
shot across the sky

the stones do not
speak any more
to blighted beings
lost in motion.
They wait
and sing
their hymns
of sacred sorcery –
transforming layer
by layer
this simple rock
forgotten in the
sandy bay
of hesitant stars
and certainty

first published in *Songs of Eretz Review*

discordance wanes

Rick Stassi

Discordance wanes
but words still
do not come easy.
How pondering and wondering
hold sway.
I see resonance wax
in pleasing hope
waiting to see
that part of me
where soft light-
from inward deep-
keeps me from falling.
O, how my own futile
attempts at
defeating gravity
and absolutes
leaves me in
unbalance.
But the soft light
is not so subtle!
Permeating into my being
probing soulfully:

Who am I?

It matters not
where i wish to go
or who I wish to be
as all things about me -
here and there-
are kept close to
the Creator's heart.
This causes joy
and begs illuminating thought.
All in all
we are of God and
selfish countenance
transcends to heir
and servant to give all
back now in meted increments
that which has been
gracefully given.

Pathu and a Python

FABIYAS M V

It's not a love that's creeping in her sleep.
Though wounding kisses wake her up, her
worn-out body – an old Indian make – resists.
She grabs its head as it twists around her –
both are tough fighters – loser will lose life.

The fray on her floor doesn't seem to end.
This snake coil isn't as hard as cruel arms
that had wound her youth – as rough as the coir
ropes that had bound her wrists to an iron grill.

Bite marks appear as antique art on her
arched body – her rich mistress had made similar
adornment on her back with a hot metallic bar.

She had boiled her tender emotions in a kettle
in the kitchen. She had no other way, then, but
to live as a servant in a rich ranch house. Really,
she'd no roof over her life – an orphan's always
exposed to the pain drops and memory light.

They are lying like two wrestlers on a torn mat.
Pathu's yell goes out through the cracks in her
walls. Neighbors gather – enjoy the game –
indicate her heroism – take photos – share them on
Whats App and Facebook. Finally, they rescue her.

They unwind and leave the python in the nearby
wood amidst the hullabaloos. Stomachs of their
cell phone cameras are full. Since she has no
poisonous thoughts, she curls up in serenity again.

Published in the latest issue of *Shooter Literary Magazine*

Mermaids Are Waiting For You!

Martin Elster

It sat there on the strand that day,
  a day that viewed strange meetings.
He picked it up from where it lay
on grit and pebbles, wet from spray,
  bruised by the breakers' beatings.

He held it up against an ear,
  an ear drenched by the thunder
of muted oceans, far and near —
a pink-lipped conch, a souvenir
  he thought, until from under

its briny, salmon-colored sound,
  a sound unlike the ocean:
a voice that told him it was bound
to whale and seal, and never drowned,
  except in strong emotion.

"Let's meet beyond the reef," it purred,
  those purring tones erotic
as Amphitrite's, every word
exotic as a coral-bird,
  each sea-lynx growl hypnotic.

The bathers, boats, the heavens' eye
  (an eye half-closed and Titian),
rendering the western sky
so roseate, its hues would vie
  with a Turner exhibition,

to him were distant as the flight,
  the flight of a shearwater.
"I am a mermaid of the night,
whose tail is fashioned to excite.
  I frisk with eel and otter."

Waves drummed, but he just heard that arch,
  that arch, coquettish timbre.
He thought he heard the wedding march
by Mendelssohn. No hint of starch
  in that coy voice. "I'm Amber."

While plovers piped and seagulls squawked —
  squawked like the world's noisemakers —
and other seabirds plunged or flocked,
he chucked that ornate shell and walked
  straight into the breakers.

Out past the reef he met his fate,
  a fate with flowing tresses.
The sea-beast didn't hesitate
to wrap her tail around her date
  and drown him in caresses.

Originally appeared in *Scarlet Literary Magazine*

two trails of frozen footprints going in opposite directions

John Reinhart

ice cubes in eye sockets
tears freezing to grey stubble
heartbroken yeti

clouds

Rick Stassi

O disdain so sleight and lurking
presently on demeanor working
soft darkness of the under-cloud
here not seen sun's shine so proud
the grimace of another day
puts smile on hold in rapt display
and cherish comes in arms so wide
dreaming of a cloud's other side.

a warm day hidden among winter's

B. Flynn

for a moment, the sun came by,
  after a spell of colder days,
and warmed the hands t'were at my side.
  sent the striped skunk from where
  - he lays

while I thought of squandered chances
  and gentle brushes from her hair,
lost among winter's long glances
  that keep the oak and elm
  - so bare.

The Consumption of Plath

tinabarnt

This fire,
extinguished many
times before,
burns deep within
and can no
longer be ignored.

I have given
them
warm milk
and tea and honey
and set them
off to play.

For it has been decided--
today is the day.

Noxious air
will soon consume
me and at
once I will be free.

There are those
who will cry,
flowers will wilt
in my name
but the ashes
will always glow.

And the bees--
they will remember,
for I am their
queen now
and forever.

A Money Order to Tamil Nadu

FABIYAS M V

His brain's barren like
the surface
     of the moon – alphabet
could never
     grow there. I fill up the
money order
     form at his request. Our
 tongues are
     diverse –doesn't matter –
necessity fumbles
     and finds its way. He's
one of the
     inter-state coolies sweating
for our state.
     I decode the signals from
his mind –
     he's soft within a hard shell
like a coconut.
     He stares at the strange
words falling
     from my nib. He rewards
me with a
     smile like a cashew nut.
His 'thanks'
     drops into my mind, and
makes a sweet
     ripple. It's an illiterate, who
truly values letters.

(Tamil Nadu and Kerala are neighboring states with different mother tongues in India.)

First published in *The Literary Hatchet* by Pear Tree Press, US.

global warming initiative 2016

John Reinhart

gossamer flames
lace the oak
church pew
cracking varnish
not yet worn off
by a thousand pious
asses stretching time

my neighbor worships
football as I worship
flame

little suns
on earth
warm
my heart

my knuckles
crack over
the ashes
of archaim
tracing portraits:
children yet
to be born
stars long
since expired
crude cartoons

lit by flares
exhaust
pipe torches
burning the last
oil
no longer
necessary
there's so much
of society left
to burn –
this global warming
will leave no one
in the cold

First published in *On The Verge*

Stasis Dreaming

Terrie Leigh Relf

At first, it is dark in the stasis chamber. So dark that you wander through memories like black-and-white photos, but only the black appears, negative, but no positive space.

> ganglia reach out
> their tendrilled arms
> sensation

After a few hours, or perhaps it is only moments, as time moves differently in stasis, the brain and mind adjust. Vivid colors begin to seep within your dreams.

> turquoise moons
> the way starlight
> turns our flesh golden

Then, sound. . .The murmur of voices guiding you toward a doorway. Just a few more steps. . .a few more steps. . .

> neural symphony
> how the cadenza
> goes on and on

This haibun appeared in an issue of *scifaikuest*

Clarence

Bill Cushing

After a lifetime of farming,
tending land and animals,
you retired.

Replacing the rich smell of dung
with the moist scent of sawdust,
you took up hammer and chisel
to become a carpenter.
You said, half-joking,
it was the best way
to stay out from underfoot.
You told that to a reporter from Ames.

He wrote that should the Grim Reaper
ever knock on your door,
you'd invite him in for checkers
providing he was neither
a Democrat nor a Baptist;
after serving coffee,
playing a few games,
Death would leave,
a new customer.

Like many carpenters
you lost some fingers to your craft,
showing your heart
was in your work--
that sacrifice
being more important
than a few manual digits.

And the heart shows
in each finished product:
the wooden bowls
that came from a lightning-struck tree,
the clocks
all set seven minutes too slow,
or the stool
you built your great-grandson,
the seat
heart-shaped,
the legs shortened
for smaller legs.

Hamlet Had It Half-Wrong

John Reinhart

dying
one by
little
one
in my
window well,
in my
periphery,
in my
hexagonal heart –
bees
build hexagonally, exactly,
yet
mankind can find little more
than
poor four-sided collapsible
structures
based on
Euclidean
parallelism destined
never
to meet,
alone

on
one way tracks to stagnation
wherever
that may be and
yet
we be or claim to be –
it is
an important distinction –
never
quite managing
to
bee –
chamber
by chamber
of
pulsating
nectar

yearning
to
sweeten
a
right
angled
binary
world
begging
for
the light
from
a
hexagonal
window

first published in *being human*

Warmth

Tina Barnt

On a day like this
when the rain mists
and the wind blows cold,

I think about how
warm I felt as a kid,

first thing in the morning
when I'd get up and
crouch over the heat vent
that blew up my night gown
like a punch balloon.

Mom would holler for me
to get dressed and I'd
yell back that it was
too cold.

But she'd have oatmeal,
with milk and sugar
and I'd forget about
how I was about to stand
outside in the cold
waiting for the bus.

Waiting In Vain

FABIYAS M V

It's a voluntary widowhood.
Whipped by Neeli's tongue,
he's gone to harvest Dirhams*
in Dubai desert – lest the embryo
of their new home won't grow up.
She's alone in a temporary shed
behind the basement on the bank.

Indian Postman passes by like her
days flashing 'No' with his fingers.
She looks into the distant desert
through the window of nostalgia.
Fear creeps on the walls of her
heart at night - even a Norway rat
becomes a ghost rattling in kitchen.

Years slip into the chasm of past
leaving behind the doldrums on her
countenance. Time partitions her
basement – mongooses, bandicoots
and rats get their shares – holes and
chinks. Now her dreams with streaks
of love have shrunk like her womb.

*Dirham – currency of the United Arab Emirates

First published by Encircle Publications, US.

Against the Dark

Ron Sparks

in the center
of my garden of thought
is an
   inky black pool
an obsidian mirror that ripples
   and grows
with each
     and every
hurt, pain, and torment I endure
circling the pool
   my verdant hopes
   my violaceous loves
   my carmine furies -
their blooms crawl, intertwine, creep
 in a mass of emotion and impulse
    pushing ever against the center
where my garden meets that
   ebony pond;
a barren desolate blight
 of decay and hopelessness
the vivid chromaticity of my
   emotion
in perpetual campaign against
     the void
    that forever
  threatens to
      consume
      me

Windswept

Terrie Leigh Relf

how we rose
on the wind
red umbrellas
turning inside out
like solar sails
reaching for
the luminous embrace
of escape velocity
until gravity turns
outside in
returns us to the
boardwalk
by the shore.

Genesis

Meggie Royer

When Noah cleaved the water with his ark
he expected the animals to save him.
Once, my mother convinced me a c-section
was just Moses parting women's inner seas,
that magic thrived in the things
we didn't know how to name.
It was always breaking something
that undid you.
The coke into lines with the blade,
a heart, the horizon, the yolk.
Back at detox I knew
you wished to find a way back in
to the place she birthed you from,
to stay quiet like a stone
in the belly of an ocean.
We expected you to save yourself too
and in the end it flooded.

Biographies

Jamey Bibbee, a native Texan, now living in Tennessee with her husband and children. She enjoys writing poetry as a pastime. This is her first publication.

Josh Brown is a writer living in Minneapolis, MN. His work has been featured in *Fantasy Scroll*, *SpeckLit*, *Star*Line*, *Scifaikuest*, *Beechwood Review*, and more. He served as guest editor for issue 21 of *Eye to the Telescope*, the official online journal of the Science Fiction Poetry Association (SFPA). His tweets can be found at @joshbrown2778.

Julia Katherine Carrigan is thirteen-years old and lives in Glassboro, NJ. She maintains a poetry blog at juliasworld.info. Julia is completing her eighth grade year at Friends School Mullica Hill, where she learned to love poetry, with many wonderful teachers like T. Erica, T. Corri and T. Debbie, and will continue her education at George School the following year. Julia aspires to become a poetic and fantastical writer with eight cats. She would love to hear your feedback, and can be contacted via email at poetrycat818@gmail.com.

Paul Cotterill lives quietly in Lancashire, England, not too far from where he was born and bred. He got there via London, Algeria, Bangladesh, Tanzania and few other places in between. He likes to go the long way round. He aspires to the spontaneous poetic creativity of Arthur Rimbaud, but finds cheap cider a poor substitute for absinthe. He reads Jürgen Habermas and Bonnie Honig, and thinks he understands them. He tweets as @bickerrecord, but has failed to grasp any other form of social media other than shouting.

Bill Cushing has lived in several states in the Northeast and South as well as the Virgin Islands and Puerto Rico before moving to California. As an undergrad, he was named the "blue collar" poet because of his years working primarily as an electrician on oil tankers, naval vessels, and fishing boats. He earned an MFA in writing from Goddard College in Vermont and teaches at East Los Angeles and Mt. San Antonio colleges. Published in various literary journals, magazines, and newspapers, he has poems in two recently-released anthologies, *Getting Old* and the award-winning *Stories of Music,* and is slated to have another in volume 2 of *Stories of Music*. He recently had short stories appear in *Newtown Literary Journal*and *Sediment*. Bill is now collaborating with a musician on a project called "Notes and Letters," and he invites anyone interested to check out (and perhaps join) their Facebook page.

Lexi Davis was born and raised in the town of Norwood, North Carolina. She enjoys anything artsy, different genres of music, outdoor adventures, and she's a bit of a nerd with her addiction of anything of the printed word. She found her love for writing at an early age when she realized she had a gift for song writing. With help from high school English teachers, her writing ability grew and so did her love for her craft. She went on to co-writing a song for Grammy winning artist Ne-Yo when she was only 16. After finding much success, she hopes to continue it by working on what would be her debut book. You can find more of her works on Twitter: @Songz_OfMyLife and Instagram: @words_est1991.

Ebonee Eleby grew up in Sherman, Tx. She now lives in Dallas, Tx with her partner. She enjoys spending time with friends and family making memories.

Martin Elster is a composer and serves as percussionist with the Hartford Symphony Orchestra. His poetry has appeared in *Astropoetica, Cahoodaloodaling, The Chimaera, The Rotary Dial, Soundzine,* and in the anthologies *Taking Turns: Sonnets from Eratosphere, The 2012 and 2015 Rhysling Anthologies, New Sun Rising: Stories for Japan, Eccentric Press Poetry Anthology (Volume I),* and *Poems for a Liminal Age,* among others. His poem, "My Dream of Being a Leaf-Cutter Ant," was a co-winner of Rhymezone's 2016 poetry contest, "Walking With the Birds and the Bones Through Fairview Cemetery," placed first in the Thomas Gray Anniversary Poetry Competition 2014, and his poem, "The Comet Elm," was awarded third place in the Science Fiction Poetry Association's 2015 poetry contest.

Rod Kok is a Canadian poet. He currently works in the IT industry, specializing in Education. His hobbies include digital art and drumming. He looks up to anyone taller than him, but looks down on nobody. He stands 6'7. Follow him on Twitter: @rod_e_kok

Suzanne Kosmerl grew up in Buffalo, but now lives near Atlanta. She has two boys, a dog and a husband. Music, movies and books are her favorite escapes and writing keeps her sane. She blogs at The Head Writers and can be tweeted at @suzannekosmerl.

Mary Soon Lee was born and raised in London, but now lives in Pittsburgh. She has won the Rhysling Award and been nominated for the Elgin Award for her poetry. "Brighid" is part of her epic fantasy in verse, more of which may be read at http://www.thesignofthedragon.com

Fabiyas M V is a writer from Orumanayur village in Kerala,India. His fiction and poetry have appeared in several anthologies, magazines and journals. His publishers include Western Australian University, British Council, Poetry Nook, Rosemont College, US, Forward Poetry, Off the Coast, Silver Blade, Pear Tree Press, Zimbell House Publishing LLC, Shooter, Nous, Structo, Encircle Publications, and Anima Poetry. He won many international accolades including Merseyside at War Poetry Award from Liverpool University, U K, the Poetry Soup International Award, USA and Animal Poetry Prize 2012 from RSPCA (Royal Society for the Prevention of Cruelties against Animals, U K). He was the finalist for Global Poetry Prize 2015 by the United Poets Laureate International (UPLI), Vienna. His poems have been broadcast on the All India Radio. He has an MA in English literature from University of Calicut, and a B Ed from Mahatma Gandhi University.

Shauna Osborn is a Numunuu (Comanche)/German mestiza artist, researcher, and wordsmith. She has earned a BA from the University of Oklahoma and an MFA from New Mexico State University. Her debut poetry collection Arachnid Verve focuses on the acrobatic nature of Southwestern life. Shauna's list of honors includes a 2015 Artist in Residence for A Room of Her Own Foundation's Waves Writing Retreat, a National Poetry Award from the New York Public Library, Alternating Current Press Luminaire Award for Best Poetry, and the Native Writer Award from UNM Summer Writers' Conference. You can find her work online at shaunamosborn.wordpress.com.

An arsonist by trade, **John Reinhart** spends his spare time gluing things together. He lives on an urban farmlette in Colorado with his wife and three children. He is a member of the Science Fiction Poetry Association and a Frequent Contributor to the Songs of Eretz Poetry E-zine. His chapbook, "encircled," is available from Prolific Press. You may find more of his poetry and links to yet more at http://www.patreon.com/johnreinhart and connect with him at https://www.facebook.com/JohnReinhartPoet.

Terrie Leigh Relf lives in San Diego, CA, and is a lifetime member of the SFPA, an active member of the HWA, and the contest judge for Alban Lake Publishing's drabble contest. Recent poetry collections include *Search for a Kinder Muse* (Smashwords, 2015), *An Untoward Bliss of Moons* (Alban Lake Publishing, 2015), and *Letting Out the Demons and Other Poems* (Elektrik Milk Bath Press, 2014). She was also one of the participating poets in *Confessions: A Nightmare in Five Acts,* edited by Joshua Gage (Elektrik Milk Bath Press, 2014). Relf is the author of *Poet's Workshop - and Beyond!* (Alban Lake Publishing, 2012). Please visit her websites at tlrelf.wordpress.com and terrieleighrelf.com for more information and to sign up for the *Kinder Muse Newsletter* et al.

Rie Sheridan Rose is the author of five chapbooks of poetry. Her poems have been published in Penumbra, The Voices Project, and Wolf Willow magazine, as well as the Boundless, Metastasis, Twenty: In Memoriam, and Di-Verse-City anthologies. She has had poetry in Terror Train, Bones II, No Sight for the Saved, and Abandoned Towers as well. Her first poem performed in public was written in the third grade, and she has been writing poetry and performing it ever since. She is also a lyricist.

Ron Sparks (1970 -) is a poet and science-fiction and fantasy author. He has a deep love of haiku, cinquain, and free verse poetry. Among his poetic influences is Basho, Issa, Charles Bukowski, Allen Ginsberg, Maya Angelou, and many others too numerous to detail. In addition to poetry projects, Ron is currently working on the next book in his sci-fi series, a new dystopian future book, and a non-fiction book about his cancer. Ron also enjoys motorcycle riding, astronomy, martial arts, scuba diving, whiskey, traveling, and spending time with his wife and three children. Ron currently resides in Pittsburgh, PA and in Orlando, FL. To find out more about Ron and his published works, visit http://www.ronsparks.com.

Meggie Royer is a writer and photographer from the Midwest who is currently majoring in Psychology at Macalester College. Her poems have previously appeared in *Words Dance Magazine, The Harpoon Review, Melancholy Hyperbole,* and more. She has won national medals for her poetry and a writing portfolio in the Scholastic Art and Writing Awards, and was the Macalester Honorable Mention recipient of the 2015 Academy of American Poets Student Poetry Prize.

Steve Shultz lives in Denver, Colorado with his family. He is the author of two books of poetry, *FM Ghost* and *3: Poems for My Wife and Kids*. His work has been published in various anthologies and magazines both online and in print. Music and film are a few of his other obsessions. Read more of his work at https://fmghost.wordpress.com.

Rick Stassi was born and resides in Sacramento California. His interest is in music and art. He is married to Dana and has two children, Blake and Phoebe. God inspires all things and He is love. Words can only attempt to show this.

Lynn Tait is an award-winning poet and photographer residing in Sarnia, Ontario Canada. He poems have appeared in literary journals in the U.S. and Canada. She has been published in over 70 anthologies and her photos and photo art has graced the covers of various poetry books and anthologies. She is a member of the League of Canadian Poets and The Ontario Poetry Society. She has published a chapbook, "Breaking Away" and a book with 4 other Canadian poets "Encompass I".

www.ingramcontent.com/pod-product-compliance
Lightning Source LLC
Chambersburg PA
CBHW020554030426
42337CB00013B/1098